The Good Truth

poems by

R.B. Simon

Finishing Line Press
Georgetown, Kentucky

The Good Truth

Copyright © 2021 by R.B. Simon
ISBN 978-1-64662-538-3 First Edition
All rights reserved under International and Pan-American Copyright Conventions. No part of this book may be reproduced in any manner whatsoever without written permission from the publisher, except in the case of brief quotations embodied in critical articles and reviews.

ACKNOWLEDGMENTS

"wind" and "indelible" first appeared as previous versions in *Anti-Heroin Chic*
"Reflections on Geese Flying South" first appeared in *Blue Literary Journal*
"Second Harvest" first appeared in *Literary Mama*
"thirst is angry at water" is from the poem "The Self We Share." © Mewlana Jalaluddin Rumi
"who are you,little i" is from the poem by e.e. cummings of the same name. © e.e. cummings
"Marriage Advice" first appeared in *Bramble Literary Magazine*
"Prairie Fire" first appeared in *Cutleaf Journal*

Publisher: Leah Huete de Maines
Editor: Christen Kincaid
Cover Art: R.B. Simon
Author Photo: Kandra Shefchik
Cover Design: Elizabeth Maines McCleavy

Order online: www.finishinglinepress.com
also available on amazon.com

Author inquiries and mail orders:
Finishing Line Press
PO Box 1626
Georgetown, Kentucky 40324
USA

Table of Contents

Heritage 1

Traditions 3

schools 4

Rosendale, WI 1981 6

who are you, little i? 8

The Graduation of Fatty Patty 9

She Was Wrong 11

Prayer for the Unknowable 12

Thirst is Angry at Water 13

anything to keep you happy 14

Reflections on Geese Flying South 15

Marriage Advice 16

Prairie Fire 17

Creeping Charlie 18

Retreat 19

Meditation 20

Wind 21

Indelible 22

Lightning 24

Second Harvest 25

Reflection 26

At 48 27

The Good Truth 28

*For Dannee and Noelle, who are my truth.
And for Lisa Marie, my wise cheerleader,
with undying gratitude.*

Heritage

I.
I was never born.
Like my ancestors, my body parts
      originated in the secret hearts of caves,
      washed from the sediment of lake beds,
bubbled up from mud pits,
      dripped from slick stalactites in echoing caverns, or
           blew down from lands of clouds and wind.
Maybe my limbs emerged whole and glistening from the sea,
      spawned across continents:
a toe from Britannia,
legs from West Africa,
ears from the high moors of Scotland,
eyes from the driftless American Midwest,
         and then
squirmed and thumped, traversing land masses,
    to be wedded at the
      alter of miscegenation
  in defiant disambiguation.
My body should babble to you in its mother tongues, but
never utter a unified voice.

II.
No one knows if the Mayflower held any of my relations;
if my twenty times great grandfather's haggard hands beat drums
or ploughed earth,
if my
great
great
great
great
grandmother's hide-wrapped feet shuffled the soil
of tear-choked trails and lamented the loss of her
only-imagined great grand-baby.

How could she
have imagined a granddaughter who was
    everything
        and nothing,
lonesome, belonging to no one
(for who can claim kinship with a bone, an organ, a swath of flesh?)
Bred across barriers,
the entire planet is my homeland
    but I claim no home.

III.
I was always taught that mutts are the smartest of canines.
But they are still mutts,
    mixed breeds.
Just like me, they have no pedigree,
carry no quorum card, no approving seal
    reading one-half hound, one-seventh schnauzer.
It is not possible to be
quadroon,
octoroon.
I am not
one-twentieth of a person.
I am a slender, barely visible bough
    of the family tree,
        buffeted and bending,
            as winds of purity whip around the branches
murmuring my name
    and gusting onward.

Traditions

My mama, white as the porcelain
bird she kept on the shelf in the living room,
my mama crooned me lullabies, stroked my hair,
rings of silky curls, never nappy like daddy's,
my mama fanned my locks across the corduroy pillow,
sang with her sweet lilt of everlasting mama love.

    She never sang me gospel songs,
    never taught me of my ancestors.

My mama taught me all people are created the same.
She told me to be color-blind, all blood runs red.
My mama was a feminist and told me
women deserved the same pay as men.
My mama taught me to fight for civil rights for gays,
for anyone different from me, but never to see differences.

    She never made me soul food,
    never cooked me collard greens or grits.

My mama taught me "proper" English
because it was all she knew how to speak.
My mama showed me how to pay attention:
how billboards used women's bodies to sell cars,
how they marketed tennis shoes to young black men
who couldn't afford them, using metaphors of war.

    She never told me the stories of Nefertiti or Langston or Rosa,
    never showed me any footprints to follow but her own.

My mama defied her entire clan to marry outside her race,
at the ripe old age of eighteen dared miscegenation.
My mama was disowned by the richest, brightest branches
of our family tree, became the whitest of the black sheep,
skulked home to a brooding mother, hungry babe in arms
when that no good negro ran off with the next blonde lady.

    She never told me a black man had broken her heart.

She never had to.

schools

round-shouldered on a windless day, alone on the swing set,
little brown girl hangs, toe tips scratching blacktop.
she pretends not to notice the approach of the predators.

hey! they call. they know her name, but never use it.
heat floods her face like boiling water, pavement so hot vapor zig-zags
across the concrete field as schoolchildren mill in pods

screeching and laughing in games of tag and kickball,
the amoeba-like pattern of them netting the full attention
of the teacher who never sees her.

hey, brown crayon! burnt toast! what's the matter?
did you know your mama left you in the oven too long?
taunts sting like electric eels across the back of her neck.

they surround her, the piranhas of the playground, as she wonders
if she will stand or bolt, heat and resignation holding her fast.
there is no more sanctuary in the school than in the wide world she flees.

hey, nigger-girl, where you from? africa? why you come here?
she has no answers for them, never answers, has learned the hard way
it's better to remain silent than hook her own mouth on defense.

tears prick, but she clamps her eyes defiantly. oh look!
zebra girl is gonna cry! laughter ripples through the group.
the stinging behind her orange-lit eyelids grows.

she stands, opening her eyes to slits to find a way through,
sees none. her feet melt to the pavement in dismay.
laughter wells up again, closer now, they are tightening the circle.

panic belches up, then a jolt—the shrill of the recess bell.
she stays, rooted like seaweed, until all the kids have run inside,
then drags her heavy body through the thick embarrassment.

returning to the door, a teacher awaits her, scowling.
you are always so slow! why don't you exercise? she knows
she cannot win their games, but nods, and follows the current.

Rosendale, WI 1981

The galloping downbeat from the
   'Mistress of the Dark' pinball machine's
     background music
  pounds through the soles
of my sand-and-pebble-filled sneakers.

Orange Nehi soda
  clutched in my grubby
10-year-old hand
    like the goldfish prize
      at a county fair;
  it's florescent sweet
    imbibed in
desperate swigs, from a bottle
  held with just one pointer
    finger around the neck,
like the grown-ups
    sitting a few feet away
  at the laminate-topped
bar counter.

Amidst the country twang
  they line the long narrow bar
    like birds on a wire,
 feet propped on the bottom rungs
   of the red vinyl and chrome barstools,
farm boots covered
  in mud and cow shit,
their deeply tanned muscles framed
  by sleeveless sweatshirts
      all in the same overbleached grey knit.

    Labor-roughened hands
        lift sweating brown beers
  to sun chapped lips, crook-fingered,
        while they talk
            in grown-up mutters
        too low to warrant
my pre-adolescent attention.
    But always I stand
cocked, one-eyed, towards them
          positioned just so
  between the bar and
        my younger cousins
            playing pinball next to me.
Always I note who is swaying,
            who is slurring first.

Mistress Elvira peers down at us
    lights flashing all around
her bouffant of jet-black hair,
        smiles obliging, amused,
as if she is just about to start laughing,
as one by one, the farmers lean away
    from the sticky faux wood top and empty bottles,
      jingling keys in hand, beckoning the youngsters
           into buckle-less backseats of rusting pickups,
    sticky fingers pressed against glass
in silent farewell.

who are you, little i?

peeking out the second story window across
the driveway to the neighbor girl's house,
hoping for a flash of friendly face. *who are you?*
watching fireflies evade the boys with the mason jar
prisons, flicking their bottoms in wanton displays

of joy. shoulders hooked in a quilted baby blanket,
tucked far to the back of your walk-in closet,
clinging to fantasy novels of imagined worlds
like the ivy vines beneath your window,
dragons, fairies, the dashing cavalier

vanquishing the villain in every same-old story.
who can you be? hidden away from even yourself
inside this teddy bear-lined cave, mind blank of
all it has witnessed, aching with a searing
sadness, a loneliness you have no words for?

keep gazing, little i, out the window into the
night. the soft yellow rays of the sun will clamber
their way above the horizon come dawn.

The Graduation of Fatty Patty

The words inside the cookie
were as bland as the Chinese
food that preceded them,
which is to say I don't recall them,
only feeling too mortified to
end it with 'in bed' with my parents
at the table, quite possibly the only
thing that would have made
the meal entertaining.

Truthfully, I'd come only for the
chow, addicted to any substance
capable of numbing (and as yet
unfamiliar with the faster and far
more reckless methods I would
discover in my later years.)
I had no eagerness for what was
to follow and lingered over watery
diet soda dregs before heaving
myself to the sputtering
late model sedan outside.

I was wilting in the sultry 90s, humid
heat, too embarrassed by my 200-plus
pound, dimply teen body to wear anything
revealing, baking in my white knit pants
with tiny black hearts, pilled from
repeated washing (because my step-father
didn't believe in a bigger back-to-school
budget just because plus sized cost more.)
At the school, glinting silver bleachers bulged
with parents in summer finery, scanning
for their Purple Knight on the field below.
Mine joined them as I squeezed miserably
past knees and toes to my spot, feigning
no notice of the glares and giggles.

Superintendent and Principal lauded
the valedictorian, the key note, the
Teacher of the Year. As whistling
and hooting began, each Knight crossing
the stage, my stomach somersaulted,
risking placement of all the
previously ingested Chinese food.
I joined the line—feet dragging, eyes down—
for the looming, scaffolded stage.

Audience applause metered each
student's family influence and
general popularity with thunderous
cheers or polite golf patters.
But as my plump sandaled toe
grazed the steps, the sounds
of adoration stilled, until at last
I could hear the straining of my
sainted mother's furious clapping,
feigning an entire army of parents.

Crossing the endless plywood
in front of the eerily placid town
a zealous gust of summer breeze
whipped the front of my eggplant frock
skyward, exposing my wretched worn pants,
unshaved kneecaps, and face-burning shame.
I snatched the meaningless diploma, bolting
for the other side of the infernal platform.

The rest of the ceremony blurred
as my attention laser-focused on the
roiling humiliation in my abdomen.
While preening grads posed for snapshots
with doting relations, I dashed indoors,
gratefully reaching the mint-and-Pepto
tiled bathroom, slamming shut the far stall,
letting fly the coveted feast, praying
between heaves to the god of porcelain
to deliver me from my youth.

She Was Wrong

    After I delivered the news
sitting across the kitchen table
    at age nineteen,
      mom wept softly,
  whispered that the world was too cruel;
How would I ever be happy again?
    She could not have seen this:
  the way you turn in your sleep,
      arm wrapping by habit
    around my waist, face pressing against
the back of my neck in an unspoken
      I love you.

Prayer for the Unknowable

Lately, I am compelled
   to press bare knees to carpet
     head stacked on steel-clasped hands
contemplating the Great Unknowable,
   trying to grasp the marvel that wrought
this fragile miracle,   created in the
   inviolate force of beating organs synched in lurching rhythm, and
   the excruciating dichotomy of tenderness and ardor
that decants from our skin singing together in sweeping caresses.

   These ablutions we perform for each
   are nothing if not sanctified.

   If there is an answer
 I have never found it in my solitary churning reflections,   or the
      questing of my slumbering psyche.
    Relief is only in the sighing respite found as my body slides
into the empty
space next to yours,
   ionized like two seeking magnets.
     In leaning into your two open hands,
       and surrender.

Thirst Is Angry at Water

You pass by me
close, again,
for the umpteenth time today,
wanting only to be near me,
breathe kisses into the vee of my neck,
until I push you away like a
drunken sailor in wartime, glaring
a warning from under pinched brows,
eyes spinning a familiar *do-not-cross* barrier
across the length between us.

At night, you squeeze around my back, hard
but careful not to trip alarms with your stray hands before
rolling over, descending swiftly into stone sleep. Leaving
us like mismatched bookends, one with eyes open,
shining dully in the dark, for no one to notice.

anything to keep you happy

it was the way I always woke before you,
placed one cautious foot to carpeted floor,
folded back blankets careful not to wake you,
slid through an inched open bedroom door
out to the living room balcony for my first cigarette,
breathed out over treetops wondering which one
of you I would encounter today, until I sensed
your footsteps, braced for the opening volley, and
stacked facial muscles into
a good morning

Reflections on Geese Flying South

What freedom
    there must
        be in taking
            wing away from
        what instinct
      says will
    starve you
s l o w l y.

Marriage Advice

Last night after a fight with my lover
I sat on my front porch under an umbrella,
vicious thunderstorm pounding
down around me, tugging
the umbrella slantways
and shaking, as I smoked my cigarette
angrily, watching the park across the
street light up with electric daylight.
It felt like Mother Nature laughing, as the
storm grew more furious and insistent,
clucking her thunder-tongue in a mighty show,
sending her rain slivering sideways
beneath my umbrella like finger pokes:

    Girl, you know nothing of storms,
    go put your petty squall to bed.

Surrendering my anger to the gale,
returning inside to lover quiet,
stretched out on the bed, I strip
off my clothes sodden with Her teaching,
lay down, offering my tongued apologies,
lover rubbing raindrops into my skin
like holy oils, and outside, the rain slowed,
and the moon broke through.

Prairie Fire

Each year, the placard tells us,
   Ho-Chunk Indians
     burned this prairie to ash,
    rooting out invasive species—
       the buckthorn and the honeysuckle,
         so eager to conquer
           and upend precarious order.

Still, when settlers came,
  with their muskets, beaver traps, plagued blankets,
larceny disguised as
       gratitude
          no cleansing burn laid clean the land
          no prairie fires
  released the seeds of a new spring
         and the ancestors' ghosts wept.

Today, trudging up sage-drab
   hillside snaked by waterways,
    lined in desiccated grasses,
   looking down on fields of
oxtail, purple coneflower, silky aster
   cleaving mightily to the
embattled substrate,
        clamoring their defiance
         in gaudy hues,
   I am thinking of how
     the Ho-Chunk know a secret:
that to destroy something so
       very precious to you,
    some part of what you call home,
is to let it return to you
   filled only with
      the essence of all
it was ever meant to be,
   black and bare,
     seeded
        and ready for spring.

Creeping Charlie (or, Late Summer, Post-Diagnosis, Pre-Hospice)
~For Lavender (In Memoriam, May 6th, 2020)

The dragonflies
dove between the
shafts of sunlight as the baby
sat in sweet swaying grass
next to the weed-packed bucket.
We'd talked hours, our labors
hardly labor, before falling into
companionable silence, gingerly tugging
the inconsiderate vines from between
the irises in Derek's Garden.
The humid earth called me back.
We chatted idly about flower transplants,
school trips. I was meticulous
with spade and glove, coaxing
the fertile soil back smoothly,
until, reluctantly, you admitted
defeat, making silent, round-eyed apologies.
You scooped up baby, offered good-bye
hugs, were swallowed by the shadows
of the cool sanctuary of indoors.
I lingered, tidying the garden,
pulling up the last of the Charlie vines.
As if everything wrong could be
rooted out, as if I could pull
it all from Mother Earth's body to
save yours, toss it all among the
compost, to spread among the irises
and grow you one more day.

Retreat

Falling stillness:
  whiteness,
peeling birch trunks
    tracing icy roadways to
      bleached heavens,
abandoned benches
  like rice long after
    the wedding,
scattered along arched
    forest pathways
     bathed in
diamond radiance.

Far off,
the echo of
  a drum circle,
    a shot of laughter,
    a door creaking,
  fades
with each brittle footfall
  away from traces
of human modernity,
  only the indiscernible
  spinning golden
    thread of
     human connection
left to tether
  one soul,
    plodding
     purposefully,
  toward the
horizon crowded with stars
  and the
    sound of
     infinity.

Meditation

Lashes interlaced
    fluttering
  the darkness floods itself with
film stills and
     fractionals,
  mirror shards like
    popcorn flung
     across the
universe of my
    inward vision,
moments tumbling as
    anguish,
     resistance,
      and finally—
  quietude
 puddles
     at the corners of my vision,
     droplets
  like grace caught
in saline.

Cradling this stillness
   is a gift
     born of
       restlessness;
the fiends and furies of
     battles hard won
       and hard lost
laid to rest
   in the cavern of
 my open aching chest.
Sighing exhalations,
      a loosening,
     a yearning quenched,
   and at long
    last—
 breath
 taken
   in.

Wind

Gusting in as furiously
    as her mother's anger
the blackberry clouds
    sending branches
flinging like air-born
    battering rams
pricking her bare arms
    like premonition
as she crosses the street,
    ducks into the half-hanging door
of the warehouse with
    it's cracked, bucktoothed façade
leering as it swallows her.

Inside, she performs
    the ablutions:
fire, spoon, cotton,
    lightning licking the wall
in stop-motion intervals
    illuminating her laddered spine,
the clockwork motions,
    anticipation slightly wobbling
the orange capped
    syringe in her hands
up until the moment
    the lightning ceases,
a crack of thunder snapping
    as she plunges down
        and down.

It takes only seconds
    for the brain to slow the breathing,
for the heart to skip
    a beat, a beat, a beat,
for froth to appear
    at the corner of a slackening lip,
for a flame
to blow out
in the wind.

Indelible

My heart has
   wound down slow these days,
     like an old wristwatch,
skips metaphorical measures
   when I think of that night,

how I kissed your spittle-flecked lips
between compressions—
   come back to me
    1 - 2 - 3
   come back to me
    1 - 2 - 3
—ruby droplets drying on your cheek.

I
could
not
save
you.

Once you were   breath   bone   cartilage.
You would think your ghost would be weightless,
   but I am so heavy with you.

Weeks after,
I found myself guiltily peering
   through your journal pages and sketches,
posthumous voyeur of your life's doodles,
the butterfly you drew
   symbol of your recovery
   swirled and labyrinthine.

Page in hand I trudged to the tattoo parlor
barely managed a whisper:
    "over my heart"
your blood   into ink
    onto bone
  needles stinging like recriminations.

Now I imagine her wings batting, lifting off,
riding my night sighs to find you,
returning to me, bearing your wordless benedictions
    worn as an amulet, against another day
      without you.

Lightning

The wife of an ex
of an old friend of mine
was once struck by lightning.

It entered through the top
of her head, traversed her whole body
to exit through the toe of her boot.

The force of the blow
exploded her lower skull.
They said she was lucky to survive.

For months after
she drank dinner through straws,
jaw wired shut from reconstruction.

Some said she was different,
something not quite the same,
but life went back to mundane.

What else does one do
when the very cells of your brain
have been shone through with sunlight?

When a fingertip of god
touches the soft tissue and reminds you:
you too, child, you too are mine?

Second Harvest

      She is such a tiny bud, raw with
winter's scrubbed potential, born to high winds
        and parents of dune thistle,
          grandparents of red baneberry,
lost in a rough country of ancestry
not recognizing oak, from aspen,
        from elder.

I want to bring her baskets of our fruit,
    bowls of blackberries or little wild strawberries just plump enough to
        crush between teeth, to burst open and stain the lips.
          I want them tart with her lineage,
            sweet with the pith of who she will become, of
        how she was rooted a thousand years ago.

      And I am no master gardener
unskilled at pruning or coaxing bud to blossom,
   I can't tell sly weed from straining sapling
        except for this one
          glorious shoot.

So, go ahead, dance, little one.
   Let your bare toes take root everywhere they will,
     let the winds shake loose your laughter
           like seeds,
      and let it
        settle, fatten, sprout,
    and seek new sun.

This is no longer
   my harvest.

Reflection

Some claim
the mirror
is silver, exact.
Floating, detached,
the lined, sallowed face
of the strange woman
before me wears my skin,
hung from my bones
like a winter coat,
grimed with the soot and salt
of the gray weather's
passing. Wears my
years like a requiem,
a token of remembrance
for what was lost
or taken.
I smile, but she only grimaces,
folds of strain
fanning from the corners
of her sunken eyes.

At 48

And now
I become myself;
a hardened
bulb of dahlia
buried under
winter's compacted earth.

Swelling with sun,
I break apart into tentacles
seeking the living air.

Bare and hot,
I raise my petaled head
and bow to the wind,
my only master.

The Good Truth

It is no accident, that when you look back
at old photos, the ones you first shunned
(thighs too fat, hair too messy)
showing your round-eyed daughter
what life was like back then, that you see yourself
differently. See there, how you threw back your head
with laughter, mouth sheltered by one slender hand.
See how your eyes were full and soft as a mare's,
how once you were unseasoned. How easy
it is to forget you are her. How easy, to forget
that it all belongs to you—the laughter,
the innocence, the fight, the ache—
how it is yours as the moon is the tide's:
an uncountable distance away,
but always there, in your
hollow, cupped hands.

R.B. Simon is a queer artist and writer of African and European-American descent. She has been creating art since her fingers first could hold crayons and writing poetry since teenage angst first hit at age eleven. She now enjoys the wealth of creativity created by exploring both visual and written elements of the expressive arts, taking great pleasure in the juxtaposition of the two. When crafting poetry, she is most captivated by the expansiveness of words, the hunt for specificity of language, and the opportunity to evoke visceral responses in a reader, aspiring to transport them into a crystallized moment in time that can be felt beyond words. Her poetry focuses on the mosaic of identity, the experiences that make us who we are in totality.

Ms. Simon has battled mental health issues, substance use disorder, and a history of trauma throughout her life. In recovery, she's become a Certified Peer Specialist, supporting others on the same journey. She is currently in undergraduate in Art Therapy and Psychology at Edgewood College. In her "free time" she enjoys reading, painting, gardening, baking, and other muggle-ish activities. Her more peculiar passions include clothing with stripes, giraffes, and coffee-flavored caffeine. She has been published in the *Terra Preta Review, The Green Light Literary Journal, Anti-Heroin Chic, Blue Literary Journal, Electric Moon, Bramble Literary Magazine, Cutleaf,* and *Literary Mama. The Good Truth* is her first book. Ms. Simon is currently living in Madison, WI with her partner, young adult daughter, and four unruly little dogs.

www.ingramcontent.com/pod-product-compliance
Lightning Source LLC
LaVergne TN
LVHW041513070426
835507LV00012B/1550